IMAGINING BRAD
AND
THE VALERIE
OF NOW

BY PETER HEDGES

★

★

DRAMATISTS
PLAY SERVICE
INC.

IMAGINING BRAD and THE VALERIE OF NOW
Copyright © 1991, Peter Hedges

All Rights Reserved

SPECIAL NOTE

SPECIAL NOTE ON MUSIC

for my mother, Carole
my father, Robert
my sister, Mary Clare

ACKNOWLEDGEMENTS

I am extremely grateful to Carole Hedges and Robert Krueger, Tom Hulce, and Tim Guinee for financing the writing of this play.

In particular I would like to thank Marc H. Glick, Jeannine Edmunds and Jeff Melnick, the Edge Theatre, Tanya Berezin and the Circle Rep, Adrienne Hiegel and Lanford Wilson. Several theaters and many actors did readings of various drafts. Their input was most valuable. So thank you to Connie Ray and James Duff, Joan Allen, Haviland Morris, Pat Nesbit, Margo Lindsey Smith, Ashley Gardner, Mary Mac, Jessica Rausch the Cab Theater Company, the Parnell Playwrights Unit at Playwrights Horizon, Larry Smith, the Manhattan Class Company, the North Carolina School of the Arts, Susan Batten and Marty Rader. And I am most grateful to all those who worked on the Circle Rep production especially designers Loy, Dennis, Laura and Stewart, stage manager extraordinaire Denise Yaney, the actresses Sharon, Erin Cressida, and Melissa Joan; Paula Hart and family, and a special thanks to the play's director, Joe Mantello.

AUTHOR'S NOTE

IMAGINING BRAD, in its brief history, has provoked various responses. One young man threw a chair at me after a staged reading. A certain critic wanted to burn the theater down. Others have been touched. One middle-aged woman with tears in her eyes said, "I was abused when I was a little girl. I've never been able to laugh about it. Thank you for letting me."

The play is delicate. If you perform it with compassion for these women, with no negative judgement, with no feeling of superiority, then you will have let them live and let the audience care. If these women are portrayed as different from you or me, if they are commented on or made into caricatures, then the audience is given permission to dismiss the play and the questions it asks.

The set can be simple. Most important, Brad must never be seen. He is to remain imaginary.

THE VALERIE OF NOW was presented as a prologue to the Circle Rep production of IMAGINING BRAD. The plays are inner-related; however, each work stands by itself. IMAGINING BRAD is most effective when performed alone.

IMAGINING BRAD

IMAGINING BRAD was produced by Circle Repertory Company (Tanya Berezin, Artistic Director; Connic L. Alexis, Managing Director) in New York City, on February 6, 1990. It was directed by Joe Mantello; the set design was by Loy Arcenas; the costume design was by Laura Cunningham; the lighting design was by Dennis Parichy; the sound design was by Stewart Werner and Chuck London; and the production stage manager was Denise Yaney. The cast was as follows:

DANA SUE KAYE .... Sharon Ernster
BRAD'S WIFE .... Erin Cressida Wilson

CAST OF CHARACTERS

Dana Sue Kaye — a thirty-one year old Nashville native
Brad's Wife — younger than Dana, new to Nashville

PLACE

Nashville, Tennessee

TIME

The present

IMAGINING BRAD

SCENE 1

The first Sunday.

Dana Sue Kaye and Brad's Wife are sitting in a church's social room, some time after the service.

DANA. Nashville is a lovely town. A romantic town, did you know that? Well, it is. Few people know it but then again I guess few people know Alex. But I know Alex. I *know* him. If you get my meaning. Now don't worry, honey, Alex is my husband. But many people don't know their husbands — many people wouldn't *want* to know their husbands. But Alex? Knowing Alex is knowing that there is a god. A merciful god, a loving god who provides wondrous miracles. I come to church not because I believe in all that crap, honey, but because I come to thank whoever or whatever brought me my Alex. A church is as good as any place to say thanks. So that's why I am here on this particular Sunday. Not because of Jesus. But you're here for Jesus, right? When you were down on your knees praying so hard and the tears were falling off your face — don't think I didn't notice this cause I did — when you were crying like that you were praying to Jesus, weren't you?
BRAD'S WIFE. No.
DANA. Hmmm. So why were you kneeling and praying ...?
BRAD'S WIFE. My husband said it would be good for me to go to church — to meet people ... to make new friends ... he was right. We met.
DANA. Uh-huh. So why were you crying?
BRAD'S WIFE. Uhm. No reason.
DANA. *Why were you crying?!*
BRAD'S WIFE. Uh. Cause.
DANA. Why, honey. Oh tell me why — tell Dana Sue Kaye

why.

BRAD'S WIFE. Cause I missed him.

DANA. Huh?

BRAD'S WIFE. I missed Brad.

DANA. Your husband, I hope.

BRAD'S WIFE. Yes.

DANA. Oh, how sweet. You missed your husband.

BRAD'S WIFE. Yes. We've only been married a month.

DANA. Believe me, honey, if you live right and love right you will feel the same in ten years. I miss my Alex. When I'm away from him. I've burst out crying even if he just walks out of the room. And you're newlyweds. How sweet. *(A beat.)* Honey, don't take this as a criticism, please, because by no means is it meant as one — but Brad should have been with you this morning at the service. He should have been here so when the pastor asked for the newcomers to stand up you would not have been standing alone. Your being here and his *not* being here makes most people — not me, mind you, makes *most* people wonder if there is something wrong or strange about your marriage. Obviously, any idiot could see that you love your husband very much — (I see it in your eyes whenever you say his name) — and I'm sure Brad is a wonderful man. A one of a kind man, I'm sure. I would just encourage you to get his little bottom into church next Sunday before the congregation gets certain ideas which I'm sure are not so.

BRAD'S WIFE. But Brad ...

DANA. Honey, I don't want to argue! I'm just offering you, *giving* you some advice on what I would do if I were you. You can take it or leave it — no sweat off the bones in my back. What I offer is just a collection of wisdom and experience that I've gathered over thirty-one years of living and thirteen god-like glorious years of marriage. Were I you, I would listen to me. Were I you. *(A beat.) Anyway.* If you were to ask me if Alex and me were a happily married couple, what do you think my answer would be? What do you think it would be? *(Brad's Wife is about to speak when.)* Y. E. S. YES! Without pause for consideration or stutter for hesitation. I am in *love* with Alex, I make *love* to Alex, we define *love* and I know you know that

12

what I say I mean. I *mean* it. Can you tell that? *(Brad's Wife nods.)* See — you're an observant person. I mean, I can tell that's why you and I have hit it off so well. I mean, let's face facts. People move into Nashville all the time. There is an influx, a veritable flood of people *pouring* into Nashville — it is one of the fastest growing regions in the south and if you doubt this then you doubt yourself — which you clearly *do not* do. Let me say this — I have the opportunity to take countless numbers of new people around town, show them the ins and outs — I'm on the welcoming committee of this church — but rarely do I uh offer my services. Beggars can't be choosy and frankly I can be choosy because I am no beggar. You caught my eye. I'm very taken by the way you obviously live your life — freely, openly, ready to embrace all that strikes and moves you — and this is good. *Very* good. *(A beat.)* Newlyweds — hmmm. Do you have a wedding picture with you? Most newlyweds do, you know.

BRAD'S WIFE. Yes.

DANA. Oh good! How I love wedding pictures. I'm what some call a wedding expert, having helped in countless marriage celebrations as a member of this church's altar guild. I'll bet you made a lovely bride.

BRAD'S WIFE. *(Extending a picture she took from her purse.)* Here.

DANA. Oooooooo — ohhhhhhhh — how nice! But honey, how odd. You're the only one in the picture. Where was Brad, taking the picture?

BRAD'S WIFE. No.

DANA. Where was he for god's sake? I'm dying to see what he looks like.

BRAD'S WIFE. Brad doesn't have pictures taken.

DANA. How silly — what is he, a vampire or something? Doesn't have pictures taken of himself — how strange. And on his wedding day, no less. What goes on with this guy? *(Brad's Wife is about to speak when.)* You must admit that my first impressions are not the kind one might call impressive — you *must* admit that ...

BRAD'S WIFE. Uhm.

DANA. Well think about it sweetie. What I know so far — and Dana Sue Kaye just knows what she has heard — I mean, believe it or not, I am not all knowing, all powerful — I'm not God — although there is God in me — I mean, I'm NOT God but I'm part God — and don't ask what parts are God and what parts aren't because *I don't know*. I just know that part of me *feels* holy part of the time. My hair, when I've washed it and blown it dry, sometimes it feels holy. The white, soft skin on my behind, smooth like a baby's bottom, unscathed by the sun, unseen by the human eye (except for Alex, of course) — my littlest toes, how they have been pushed up, scrunched into the other bigger toes — that part of me has a noble, almost holy quality. But I'm *not* all knowing and I'm glad I'm not because *then* I would have to offer advice, I'd have to counsel, I'd have to solve your problems as well as a billion or more other people's problems and frankly I just don't have the time. Time, my dear, is a thing we're out of. As a planet. *I* believe this. *So.* What am I saying? I already have my own personal reservations. About this man of yours. This Brad. This man who you've committed your entire life and being to — this man who I'm sure you throw yourself onto nightly, the man who plunges you, who fills you with his juice — this man who does not hesitate to get you on your knees and mount you — this same man just can't seem to make it to church with his beautiful young bride for their first Sunday when they are new in town. (I'd be lying if I said this was acceptable behavior.) One might suppose that he's still sleeping off a very active and passionate night of *love* making. Well, you're here. He isn't. Also, I note that this man refuses to be photographed, even on his wedding day, leaving one to suppose that perhaps his only interest is in photos of the nude kind, the pornographic kind. I mean, I don't know. These are just things a person watching might be left to wonder about. Who is this Brad? What is his story? You know what I'm saying. You know that I'm not criticizing — or judging — you know that ...
BRAD'S WIFE. Yes.
DANA. I mean, it's not my fault. I mean, had Brad been here

— had we met — had the congregation seen him stand by your side, his wedding band solidly wrapped around his ring finger — *then* these questions *would not* exist. We would rest easy and certain in your love. Reassured that values are returning to Nashville — that values had *moved into* Nashville — that Life was getting better — things were looking up. But no. Not today. Not this time. Not with Brad.

BRAD'S WIFE. I'm sorry.

DANA. Don't you apologize! *You've* done nothing wrong. *Nothing!*

BRAD'S WIFE. Brad doesn't go out in public.

DANA. Well, that will have to change ...

BRAD'S WIFE. But ...

DANA. No, it will. It must. This isn't the north where people don't talk to each other. This is the *South.* People smile and say good morning. People bathe. *(A beat.)*

BRAD'S WIFE. Well, Brad does bathe.

DANA. Isn't that sweet.

BRAD'S WIFE. He takes his baths at night. Some people like theirs in the morning. But Brad likes his at night.

DANA. Isn't that sweet.

BRAD'S WIFE. I run the water. Pour in the bubble bath. And scrub him real good.

DANA. Isn't that sweet you know when people meet Alex and me, do you know what they say?

BRAD'S WIFE. Uh. No.

DANA. Yippie. They say yippie *inside* because they sense our love, our union — and it's a good thing they do because it is the *truth* — and the truth wins out every time. Ah, yes. People don't have questions about Alex and me. They draw strength from our strength. But you and Brad, I'm afraid, have already caused quite a stir. Not that people are talking — I could just feel them saying to themselves during the sermon "Who is he? Where is he? Does he love you?" I mean, honestly, everything on the table, what is a person like me, a person who prefers good to evil, a person who *believes* in happy endings — what am I to think? *(Silence.)*

BRAD'S WIFE. Well — I need to get on ...

DANA. That's why I say ... let's get on to our respective homes and love our respective husbands because who knows when one of them could be killed in an avalanche or a tornado or be paralyzed for life. We have today. That's all we have — as nearly as I can see — unless you know any different. I mean, you're wanting to go home, right? *(Silence.)*

BRAD'S WIFE. Yes.

DANA. What? Have you got *so much* to do that you can't spend a little, tiny time with your newest and bestest friend ...?

BRAD'S WIFE. Well ...

DANA. I mean, of course, I understand if you want to get home to the man you will see probably every day for the rest of your life. You're probably a bit *concerned*. You probably find him a bit much to *trust*. And I could see why ...

BRAD'S WIFE. I trust Brad.

DANA. You do? Well, what if you go home and he's not there? Will you get suspicious?

BRAD'S WIFE. He'll be home.

DANA. But what if he isn't?

BRAD'S WIFE. But he will be.

DANA. But what if he isn't.

BRAD'S WIFE. You don't know Brad. *He will be home! (Silence.)*

DANA. Well, I can see I'm getting nowhere ...

BRAD'S WIFE. No, I hear what you're saying. All I'm saying is that Brad will be home. He never leaves the house.

DANA. Yeah, OK, whatever. *But* — give it a few years — a few months, even, and you'll start to wonder if he goes where he says he goes ...

BRAD'S WIFE. But he ...

DANA. You'll wonder why it takes him *so long* to pick up the dog at the vet — why his business meetings run past the 11 o'clock news. *Most* women experience this, honey. I say most because there are exceptions. And your eyes are feasting on one. I am an exception because I married the exceptional. Alex. He is faithful, loyal, kind and can bring me to orgasm. I know where he is. At all times. He doesn't even have to say it. I *sense* it. Presently he's away on business. Las Vegas. A very tempting town for most men. Alex is not most men. Were all

16

men Alex what a world this would be. Anyway, he calls me every night. We talk like we did when we first met. He reads the sexy parts of the bible to me, the kinky parts. And we giggle. Oh do we ever ...

BRAD'S WIFE. That sounds nice.

DANA. It is.

BRAD'S WIFE. Well ...

DANA. *Oh so you want to go home now!* Sure, we can do that ... *(A beat.)* I mean, we could also take just a *few* minutes and show you some of the nicest parts of Nashville. Kind of a tour? We could go for a spin in my wonderful, nifty car — see things that most people couldn't find in twenty years of living in Nashville — and since this is about the only weekend ever that Alex and I are apart, about the only *free* time I'll have — *since* this is the case, I thought I would offer. But. If you'd rather go home and see the man you'll be spending the rest of your life with — if you'd rather do that — then go right ahead — you are a newlywed — this nation's most precious commodity *and you say that you trust this man?!*

BRAD'S WIFE. For a little while, I guess it would be OK.

DANA. Would it? It would be just sooooo nice to show you some of the special places — give you a sense of this city's splendor, you know? I'd just like to do that for you. Make me feel *good* to know that you feel *welcome* ...

BRAD'S WIFE. I do.

DANA. What do you say we take a drive? *(Lights fade. We hear country music as if coming from a car radio. The lights come up on.)*

SCENE 2

The chairs from Scene 1 have been pushed together. They now suggest a car. Dana drives, Brad's Wife is in the passenger seat. Country music is heard playing softly on the car radio. Dana checks her make-up in the car mirror. A car horn sounds and Brad's Wife screams.

DANA. I'm not a bad driver! But the citizens of Nashville sure are. There is a history.

BRAD'S WIFE. A history?

DANA. Of excessive car crashes, of totalling ah-to-moh-beels. People here crash cars like how Catholics have children. *(A beat.)* Laugh. *Laugh! (Brad's Wife forces a laugh.)* Thank you. There is nothing like telling a sure fire funny joke as a gesture of friendship, then have that joke ignored. Nothing like that to churn up some of the ol' basic insecurities. But I'm not insecure. Am I? *(Silence. Brad's Wife turns up the radio and sings along to a woman singing a country and western song. Brad's Wife's voice is growing louder, more confident when Dana suddenly turns off the radio.)* So what would *you* like to see and do? We'll take *you* to where *you* want to go.

BRAD'S WIFE. Uhm.

DANA. Say it, this is your chance.

BRAD'S WIFE. Just one thing I *really* want to do and that is ...

DANA and BRAD'S WIFE. *(At the same time.)* See the country singing star's homes!

BRAD'S WIFE. Yes. How'd you know?

DANA. Predictable. Most people who come to Nashville want to see *"The Houses."* I, of course, was mistaken in thinking that you weren't like most people.

BRAD'S WIFE. It's just ...

DANA. Honey, don't explain it! You can't help it. It's your nature. And sad as it may be, I certainly don't care to hear you whimper and stutter about it.

BRAD'S WIFE. It's just Tammy Wynette, Loretta Lynn and ...

DANA. Honey, *if* that is what you want to see, then *of course* that is what we will do. *My God* I want you to have a happy tour. *But* all I'm trying to say is that you *seemed* to be a person that wouldn't give a good goddamn about *those* people. Of course, we can go to Hank Williams Jr.'s place, Loretta and Tammy's. I will try not to think about the time we *could* have had. My, my. The places I had in mind to show you. Some very special places that I just don't show anybody and that don't appear on any tourist map or tourist bus stop — you just

18

say the word and I'll bypass any tourist trap and go right to Nashville quality, you just say the word — just say the word — just say ...

BRAD'S WIFE.   OK, later.

DANA.   You saying that you'll see the houses later?

BRAD'S WIFE.   Yes, some other time.

DANA.   Oh, honey — you have made a very smart choice — and you know I'm going to pull right up here and show you something that I think you'll appreciate — that will illustrate my point. Look right over there.

BRAD'S WIFE.   Where?

DANA.   Over there. See? Do you see?

BRAD'S WIFE.   Just a bunch of graffiti.

DANA.   Not all graffiti is bad. I mean, I know it's a sin — graffiti — but I can't think of a *nicer* sin, can you? There. That spot. If you look right there. That one particular item. That one little wave of green spray paint and what do you see? What do you see?

BRAD'S WIFE.   Where?

DANA.   There. *There!*

BRAD'S WIFE.   I don't see.

DANA.   See my name. *Right there!* Come on, *anybody* could see that.

BRAD'S WIFE.   Oh. D. A. N ...

DANA.   D. A. N. A. + A. L. E. X.

BRAD'S WIFE.   Oh yes. I see.

DANA.   It was our high school prom. Fifteen god-like glorious years ago ... a May night ... Alex in a tuxedo ... and me in my white dress ... and flowers ... and we just ... had the time of our lives ... when we danced his knee pressed between me ... up in me ... and I got hot and tingly ... and then we were driving ... and he pulled out of a paper sack this can of paint ... and I said "Oh, Alex" and he said "Yes" and that "This was better than carving into trees" and I said "Yes" because they cut down trees but they won't cut down a bridge ... and so he took that can and sprayed our names ... and I wept ... I was a raining face ... and god ... what a night ... what a happy time ... *(A beat.)* Have you and Brad ever done anything like that?

BRAD'S WIFE. Brad loves me.

DANA. Of course but have you done graffiti? Surely he wrote your name on some desk in pen — or the inside of his three-ring notebook. Surely, he has done this.

BRAD'S WIFE. No.

DANA. Oh come on! There is not a guy on this planet — a guy with balls that has not written ...

BRAD'S WIFE. Brad can't write.

DANA. (Dana laughs.) You know it's none of my business but this guy must be terrific in bed. He must do something wonderful because I am beginning to have my *sincere* doubts about him, if you know what I mean.

BRAD'S WIFE. My mother said don't marry Brad. That's what she said.

DANA. I think I agree.

BRAD'S WIFE. She doesn't understand.

DANA. What is there to understand? You got a weird man sleeping in your bed.

BRAD'S WIFE. Brad is not weird.

DANA. You mean, Brad is a nonchurchgoing, photo-avoiding, illiterate and that this is not weird? Does Brad work?!

BRAD'S WIFE. No.

DANA. Well, excuse me for prying, but where does the money come from? Don't tell me you work.

BRAD'S WIFE. Not me.

DANA. Oh, I get it. I get it all now.

BRAD'S WIFE. I don't think you do.

DANA. Brad doesn't write because he doesn't need to. The guy has *sooooo* much money. And your walking to church, dressing that way, wearing that outfit is an attempt to try and dispel the "snob" notion ...

BRAD'S WIFE. No.

DANA. Honey, it's alright. I admire what you've done. It's not like I don't wish Alex and me were a little better off. Good for you, sweetie. Getting that money, going that route.

BRAD'S WIFE. But ...

DANA. I know there was some reason. Why didn't you just say he has money? I can respect that.

BRAD'S WIFE. But ...

DANA. I *said* I respect that.

BRAD'S WIFE. I don't love him for his money.

DANA. It is certainly fine if you do.

BRAD'S WIFE. But you're putting words in my mouth ...

DANA. Listen. *I* wish every now and then that I had married into money. But I married for *love* and Alex doesn't have a big bank account but he's got a big heart. And that's consolation enough. *You* have nothing to be ashamed of. It is Brad that I take issue with.

BRAD'S WIFE. You don't know Brad ...

DANA. And honey, not to offend, but I don't know if I *want* to know him.

BRAD'S WIFE. But ...

DANA. But what? Of course, I want to *meet* Brad. And I definitely want him to give Alex some financial pointers. I just wouldn't want to be intimate with Brad based on what you've told me.

BRAD'S WIFE. I haven't told you anything ...

DANA. Honey, please. It's really OK. You'll see. *(Silence. They drive.)*

BRAD'S WIFE. Where we going?

DANA. You'll see. *(Silence.)* The road going that way? *(Dana points.)* If we were to drive that way say fifty miles, we would come smack into Old Hickory Lake, a spectacular weekend getaway. Barbara has a house there. Mandrell. There you leave all worries behind. Alex and me have the private use of a fabulous ski boat with an eighty horse power potential. This boat is slick black and the life preservers are stylish, not those bright orange ones that make a woman look pudgy, a veritable piglet. The boat catches everyone's eye as you speed along, hopping waves and slapping down the skis. You and Brad would be more than welcome some sunny afternoon. We drink beer out of styro-foam mugs and laugh, sing some hymns. I'll bet you can ski. You're probably an *excellent* skier. *(Brad's Wife nods because she is an excellent skier.)* You must be just the most wonderful skier judging by how you nodded just then. My, my — am I the excited one now. And certainly Brad, then, must be some kind of champion, some Wide World of Sports caliber water skier.

BRAD'S WIFE. Brad can't ski.

DANA. Well, now that is a real life tragedy! But we can and must and will correct that. Alex is a wonderful instructor and with the proper tips, Brad will be cutting through the water ...

BRAD'S WIFE. But he ...

DANA. *He will pick it right up!* All a person does is take the skis, adjust the rubber shoes, slide both feet in ...

BRAD'S WIFE. Brad doesn't have feet.

DANA. *(A beat.)* Well, that's no problem — we'll just have some skis custom made — so that the stubs or stumps or whatever they call them will fit right into the skis — that's no problem ...

BRAD'S WIFE. But Brad doesn't have legs.

DANA. *(A beat, then bursts out laughing.)* Well hardy har har. You are the funny one. You are.

BRAD'S WIFE. Dana, did you hear me? *(Dana laughs hysterically. They drive. Dana turns the steering wheel and comes to a stop.)*

DANA. I want to show you this one spot, my *favorite* spot in all of Nashville. Isn't this a lovely park?

BRAD'S WIFE. It's OK.

DANA. Oh, honey — see you need to know a little history. This is where Alex and I first ... well, you see that basketball court? He was sixteen, I was thirteen and I had been watching him play basketball and he had loads of sweat dripping down his body, splashing the ground and I was ready with clean towels brought from home and Alex was sure glad to see me. The muscles in his legs were bursting out all over, his hair all dark and wet ... I knew Alex liked Coca-Cola so I had brought four bottles and Alex appreciated that very much and showed his appreciation by extending his hand and I just slid my hand into his — a perfect fit. *(Brad's Wife slips her hand into Dana's.)* Yes, just like that. How did you know? And we sat right there talking about little things — sat there so long that our hands grew together, the skin like bonded. It was as if our hands became *one* and still, I can still *feel his hand.* I can feel

his hand just clasping onto mine, bleeding into mine, *fusing into mine.* And we talked of basketball ... *(Brad's Wife covers her face with her available hand.)* Honey, what is it? What is it?
BRAD'S WIFE. Nothing.
DANA. No, you can talk to me. Talk to Dana.
BRAD'S WIFE. Your hand is so nice.
DANA. Any hand is nice. Surely, Brad has a nice ...
BRAD'S WIFE. No.
DANA. Excuse me?
BRAD'S WIFE. Brad doesn't have hands.
DANA. No?
BRAD'S WIFE. He's got bumps. Big wart-like bumps where elbows are supposed to be.
DANA. Oh.
BRAD'S WIFE. So ... I've never ... uhm ... held ...
DANA. Held hands?
BRAD'S WIFE. Not with Brad.
DANA. Oh, honey.
BRAD'S WIFE. It's not so bad, is it?
DANA. I think we need a drink. *(Lights fade. We hear country music from a juke box. The lights come up on.)*

SCENE 3

Lights up on Dana and Brad's Wife. The two chairs have been separated. A small table, covered with a red-and-white checkered cloth, is on stage. Dana and Brad's Wife are in a deserted smoke-filled bar. Music plays softly.

BRAD'S WIFE. We first met in Philadelphia. His family comes from ... old money. Old, *old* money. I was hired to do a singing telegram. It was my first day on the job and I was taken to this mansion and I thought people live this way? Well, I'd been warned in advance that this was not the uhm typical telegram experience — but I had no idea that what I was singing for was an uh — this little ball of flesh. This bag of —

this *freak*, you know? (*Silence. Brad's Wife smiles.*) So I sang. His parents were there and hundreds of relatives and Brad apparently hadn't uhm been responsive for years — just closed in and bitter — and when I saw him I could see why he had been this way. I tried not to look at him as I sang. But in no time what was at first ugly became soooo beautiful to me — and he must have felt this. Well, my song brought a flood of tears. Brad started talking again right then and there. The family couldn't believe it. And before I knew it they gave me a room in the house and a nice allowance and each morning and each evening I would sing for him. But it was Brad who proposed. Brad who chose Nashville. He thinks I can make it. He's so supportive. Loves me so much that he would move to this town far away from his family for me — because of *me*. He's so supportive. And I love him.

DANA. But ...

BRAD'S WIFE. But there are drawbacks, I know ...

DANA. I'll say ...

BRAD'S WIFE. Dana.

DANA. No, honey, there are things an armless, legless man just cannot do. Things a woman deserves. Do you hear me?

BRAD'S WIFE. But ...

DANA. The thought of you going back to that half human — (I've got to be honest.) — the thought of that leaves me so sad for you. So goddamned angry at Brad ...

BRAD'S WIFE. It's not Brad's fault ...

DANA. Of course not but he's got to understand a woman's needs ...

BRAD'S WIFE. He does. He loves me.

DANA. He can understand all he wants but what can he *do?* My Alex mows the yard, he cracks the eggs when I bake a cake. He carries in the groceries and weeds the garden and he can with his hand, through manual means, bring me to the greatest and most respectable of orgasms. Brad cannot do these things for you, honey — and you deserve these things. (*Silence.*) Do you not deserve these things? Yoo hoo!

BRAD'S WIFE. I love Brad. I love Brad I love Brad I love ~ad. I love ...

DANA. You say it so many times makes me think you have your doubts. *(Silence.)* Have a beer. *(Lights fade.)*

SCENE 4

A tight light comes up on Brad's room. It is night. Brad's Wife sings to Brad, who is never seen. She is at the foot of his bed. Her song lasts for several bars when she suddenly stops.

BRAD'S WIFE. This woman today. At church. Drove me around. Blab blab blab. About her husband. Alex. How they're so happy — how they make love — how they hold hands. And I got jealous. I can't look at them and then look at us. You know? Of course you do. I don't want to hurt you. But all I can think is who are we fooling? All I can think is what a big ... mistake ... this all is. I just needed to say that. *(She resumes her singing. She sings the best she can but soon she stops.)* I can't sing anymore. Not today. Maybe not ever. *(The lights fade.)*

SCENE 5

The second Sunday. Brad's Wife and Dana, at the church coffee hour. Dana has a bruise over her eye, her nose is taped with white gauze, her arm is in a sling. Still, though, Dana keeps on smiling.

DANA. Car accidents are always unfortunate. I mean, the *poor* car.
BRAD'S WIFE. Poor car? What about you?
DANA. Oh, yeah. The *people* in the car are also unfortunate victims. But it's the car that is the first thing hit. You know, we have a choice to get in the car or not get in — we have many travel options. The car has no choice. It is a car. I can

choose to travel by plane, train, helicopter, hot air balloon, a darn pogo stick even. I don't need to tell you this, though. You're an American. You are well aware of the freedom and privileges that we have in this country. Where else does a person have so many travel options, hmmm? Answer that with a name other than America and I'll be forced to do something crude and gross. *(A beat.)* Thank you for being my friend.

BRAD'S WIFE. Sure ...

DANA. For driving me, for getting me out of the house. For bringing me to church — cooped up like a lobster — you ever see those lobsters where they tape their claws shut and then they'll put fifteen or twenty in a tank, you ever see that?

BRAD'S WIFE. There was a grocery store back home ...

DANA. Well, those lobsters are me. I *sympathize* with those little buggers today, I do.

BRAD'S WIFE. I bet.

DANA. I *do.*

BRAD'S WIFE. I know!

DANA. You're my friend.

BRAD'S WIFE. Yes.

DANA. We've grown so close so fast, you know?

BRAD'S WIFE. Yes.

DANA. I'm not saying that we understand each other. God knows people are too complex to understand in a couple of talks. Like still, I've got no clue how you do it.

BRAD'S WIFE. How I do what?

DANA. This Brad character.

BRAD'S WIFE. Oh.

DANA. My understanding — and please correct me if I've got anything wrong — my understanding is that Brad has no feet, no legs even. He has big wart-like bumps for arms. Am I right?

BRAD'S WIFE. Yes, but there's more. Brad is legally blind. His eyes can detect light, though. His skin is flaky, crusty, and his ears, while he can hear perfectly, his ears look like cauliflower.

DANA. Oh my.

BRAD'S WIFE. He has no hair, really, except for a clump on

26

the side of his head. This hair is kind of blue.

DANA. And you married this man?

BRAD'S WIFE. Yes.

DANA. You understand that it's hard for me to picture this. I mean, here I am married to the best looking man in Tennessee. He does the yard work, he carries the groceries, and he makes love like — it sounds silly, I know — but like a *god.* I mean how do you and Brad share the chores, how can you go to the theatre, how can you make love?

BRAD'S WIFE. He can't do chores, it's true — and making love is awkward at best.

DANA. Well, let me just say that with this crash, I don't know how I could have managed if I were you. Because Alex has been a peach.

BRAD'S WIFE. I bet.

DANA. Coming home right after work, staying up with me if I've had a bad dream. He brings home fresh flowers, he brought me home a box of candy, records, tapes, movies for the VCR. Brad couldn't do these things for you, am I right?

BRAD'S WIFE. You're right.

DANA. Doesn't this scare you?

BRAD'S WIFE. Sometimes.

DANA. You ever had a black eye?

BRAD'S WIFE. Yes.

DANA. I've tried to convince Alex that black eyes are sexy. Alex thinks not. *(Responding toward the audience as if someone just spoke to her.)* I'm fine, thank you, Mary Pat! Yes. Alex wasn't feeling well today, Mary Pat! He is so upset. Not about the car! About me, his wife. His little kitty, me. No, I have a ride home, Mary Pat, thank you though! Hmmm? *This* is my ride. *(Dana puts her healthy arm around Brad's Wife.)* It is *very nice* of you to ask, Mary Pat. Next week, yes. Bye now. *(A small pause. Softly to Brad's Wife.)* P.S. — Mary Pat was left by her husband. Can you think of anything sadder? *(A beat.) But.* You were saying that you've had a black eye. How long till it went away ... ?

BRAD'S WIFE. I don't know because every time it was about to clear up, I'd get another.

DANA.   No kidding. How come so many?

BRAD'S WIFE.   The truth or what I told my mom?

DANA.   What do you think?

BRAD'S WIFE.   The t.r.u.t.h.

DANA.   *Always.*

BRAD'S WIFE.   The first black eye was on my twelfth birthday. I had gotten a new Schwinn with a banana seat.

DANA.   So you wiped out on your bike.

BRAD'S WIFE.   That's what we told my mom.

DANA.   We?

BRAD'S WIFE.   My dad and me. See, I had this party. And everybody went home, my mom took a nap and that was the first time my dad uhm fondled me. I resisted so he beat me. On my face. Sprained my arm. Cut my lip, too.

DANA.   Oh god.

BRAD'S WIFE.   This kept on for about five years until I was seventeen and my dad died. Once he wanted me to dance naked. I did and he still beat me.

DANA.   You say it so calmly. How can you say it so calmly?

BRAD'S WIFE.   Because I still can't believe it. That it happened.

DANA.   You're so matter of fact about it.

BRAD'S WIFE.   I cried enough, believe me ...

DANA.   You swear you're not lying ...

BRAD'S WIFE.   I swear. The lie was that I wiped out on my bike. Dad and me were so clever that we trashed my new birthday bike so Mom would believe us. See, Dad worked it out so it was my responsibility to keep the marriage together, my job to keep our secret a secret. But we could use the bike excuse only once. Then I used the "fell out of the tree" excuse. And by the time I ran out of excuses, my father died. My mother asked why I didn't cry at his funeral but she knew why. She knew all the time. But she was scared that Dad would leave, I guess. At the funeral she asked "Valerie, why aren't you crying?" I said "I hurt too much to cry." She said "No such thing." I said "Want to make a bet?" *(A beat.)* So — one time I wiped out on a bike. A bike I wasn't even riding. *(Brad's Wife turns to Dana.)* Oh, I'm not saying that you're lying.

(A beat.)
DANA. *(Smiling.)* I am.
BRAD'S WIFE. I'm not saying that, though.
DANA. *(Beginning to laugh.)* You know that I am.
BRAD'S WIFE. I had a hunch, yes. Your bruises look familiar.
(Dana is overcome with hysterical laughter.)
DANA. He used his fists! His teeth! He even took a stick to
me! How could he ... ?! Fuck him for this!
BRAD'S WIFE. Yes, I think so.
DANA. AAAAAAAAHHHHHHHHHH!!!!!!!!! *(Brad's Wife hugs
Dana.)*
BRAD'S WIFE. *(Looking out into the audience, speaking to them
as if they were church-goers who would have looked at Dana when she
screamed.)* It's OK. Everything is under control. Go back to your
socializing. Don't think a thing about us. Don't think a thing.
(Lights fade as Brad's Wife rocks Dana.)

SCENE 6

*Dana and Brad's Wife are back in the bar. Country music
plays softly. Two empty beer bottles sit next to Dana. She is
drinking her third. Brad's Wife is drinking a glass of milk.*

DANA. I could hog tie him ...
BRAD'S WIFE. How's that?
DANA. You tie his legs behind his back with his arms ...
BRAD'S WIFE. Yes?
DANA. Yes, I would hog tie him and then I would take like
some kind of vegetable — a cucumber, maybe, or a big fat
carrot — and I would stick it down his throat ...
BRAD'S WIFE. Just leave it there for hours ...
DANA. For *days!* I could shave his head ...
BRAD'S WIFE. Tickle him till he screams ...
DANA. Until he is so angry ... until his face is so red ... he'd
be yelling. Then I would gag him. I'd gag him so he couldn't
talk ...

BRAD'S WIFE. Good.

DANA. I would melt butter and pour it on him ... rub it all over and then coat him with sugar ... then I would spray paint ... him ... some rude color ... *(A beat.)* Pink.

BRAD'S WIFE. Or turquoise ...

DANA. I would open up his asshole real wide and I'd stuff things up it. Cologne bottles. Orange golf balls. Or tampon after tampon! Get a whole box stuck up his ass! *(Dana and Brad's Wife laugh.)* I might take a box of thumb tacks and push them into his feet.

BRAD'S WIFE. Staple his top lip to the coffee table!

DANA. One of those heavy duty staplers ...

BRAD'S WIFE. Yes ... !

DANA. Take one of his testicles ... yes ... and a vice grip!

BRAD'S WIFE. A crescent wrench!

DANA. And just tighten it up ... oh god!

BRAD'S WIFE. He would scream!

DANA. *YES!*

BRAD'S WIFE. Oh god. *(Silence as their laughing fades.)*

DANA. Drink a beer with me!

BRAD'S WIFE. Milk is fine.

DANA. Drink a beer! Come on! Share with me!

BRAD'S WIFE. OK. *(Brad's Wife drinks from Dana's beer.)*

DANA. Uhm. Alex. You'll just love this. *(Dana giggles.)* Oh boy. You know what his favorite thing is ... ? *This* will give you an idea ... oh boy ... *(Dana is laughing again.)* His. Favorite thing. Is for me. This is our ritual. I hold his. Penis. In my hands. And sing. The Oscar Meyer Weiner song. You know ...

BRAD'S WIFE. *(Singing.)* "I wish I were an Oscar Meyer weiner ... "

DANA. Yes.

BRAD'S WIFE. You're kidding.

DANA. No. Isn't that funny? Alex. He ... oh well ... *this* is what happened the other night. I came home, right? On Tuesday.

BRAD'S WIFE. Yes.

DANA. And there was this German shepherd with a big red ribbon on his neck. A beautiful dog ...

BRAD'S WIFE. That was nice of him.

DANA. Yes, that's what I thought, "How nice of Alex." I played with the dog. I made a quick list of possible names. It was a boy dog — that was clear ...

BRAD'S WIFE. So then what?

DANA. Alex comes home from work. I thank him. He sets up the movie projector — says that I got to watch this movie. So I'm thinking *popcorn* so I start to make it — he says forget the popcorn — just come and sit down. So I do. He turns on the movie and it's a pornographic movie which I just don't like watching, but Alex begs me to watch it, when onto the screen comes this bleach blonde girl and a dog. She puts her mouth down on the dog and I say "Oh, Alex" and he says "just wait." And the woman keeps going at the dog and I get up to leave, I'm wanting to throw up, Alex holds onto me and shuts the door and gets the dog and I'm putting it all together at this point. And he says something about not knocking something until you try it — and he's screaming for me to do this. And well there are other stories ...

BRAD'S WIFE. Oh Dana.

DANA. You know, you put up with it cause you think "it's a phase." You let your face be a punching bag for so long, your body some experimental science lab for so long and then one day you just burst — isn't that right?

BRAD'S WIFE. That's right.

DANA. I guess I just burst. But I feel better now.

BRAD'S WIFE. Does he ever just hit you, for no reason?

DANA. Well, there must be a reason, right?

BRAD'S WIFE. Not necessarily.

DANA. There must be. I must be doing something wrong. Talking too much, probably, huh?

BRAD'S WIFE. No one deserves ...

DANA. *(Interrupting.)* I know he loves me. Deep down I know that.

BRAD'S WIFE. No.

DANA. He does. I'm certain of it.

BRAD'S WIFE. That's not love. That's something else.

DANA. What is it, then?

31

BRAD'S WIFE. I don't know. It's just not love.

DANA. So what are you saying? That *you know* and *I don't know.*

BRAD'S WIFE. Yes, that's what I'm saying.

DANA. You who are married to a freak of nature, a bag of flesh ...!

BRAD'S WIFE. Brad is no freak. He's no bag.

DANA. Yeah?

BRAD'S WIFE. You don't know! *(Silence.)*

DANA. I don't need to.

BRAD'S WIFE. Brad never hurts me. Never hits me. Never forces me to do anything I don't want to do.

DANA. But he has no arms, no legs ...

BRAD'S WIFE. I know what he doesn't have, thank you very much!

DANA. The list of missing parts is ...

BRAD'S WIFE. *I KNOW!* But I would take what he gives and can't give over what you're Alex doesn't give and won't give any day of the week. *(Silence.)* It's late.

DANA. Stay, stay, stay.

BRAD'S WIFE. I've been away all day.

DANA. *PLEASE!*

BRAD'S WIFE. You've had too much to drink.

DANA. Who says? *(Brad's Wife stands.)* Don't take me home. I'm not ready yet.

BRAD'S WIFE. Let's go.

DANA. Brad isn't real, is he? You made him up, right? Hey. He is the ultimate man, right? No arms to hit you, no legs to kick. Can't see to know if you're ugly or getting older. Only words. Kind words to say you're fine. To say you're nice. To compliment. To smell your perfume. *(A beat.)* But Brad doesn't really exist, does he? No way could there be someone like him — no way is there some guy out there like him. No way. Am I right? Am I right?!

BRAD'S WIFE. Brad is real.

DANA. Do you swear?

BRAD'S WIFE. I swear.

DANA. It's hard to imagine.

BRAD'S WIFE. I know. It seems unbelievable. But there are stranger things. Nothing is quite as loving though. Loving as Brad.

DANA. Let me see him, please.

BRAD'S WIFE. No.

DANA. Let me see him so I can believe. Please.

BRAD'S WIFE. No, you'll do something cruel.

DANA. No! I won't, I swear! Let me see him, please! I want to believe. I've got to believe! Let me see him. *(Silence.)* I knew it! You're making him up! *(Blackout.)*

SCENE 7

The light comes up revealing Brad's Wife and Dana looking down on Brad's bed.

DANA. Oh god.

BRAD'S WIFE. See.

DANA. I don't believe this.

BRAD'S WIFE. Shhhh. He's a light sleeper.

DANA. He's ...

BRAD'S WIFE. Gentle.

DANA. I can see that.

BRAD'S WIFE. He loves me.

DANA. I'm sure.

BRAD'S WIFE. He loves my singing. Supports me.

DANA. You must be good.

BRAD'S WIFE. I'm better than I was. Brad makes me better.

DANA. How sweet.

BRAD'S WIFE. He makes me want to be better. *(Silence.)*

DANA. I thought he'd be grotesque. *(Silence.)* But he's beautiful. His flaky, crusty skin. It's like Christmas cookies. And the way he breathes those little short breaths ... *(Silence.)* Oh god, I feel better.

BRAD'S WIFE. I'm glad.

DANA. Thanks.

BRAD'S WIFE. So you see, there's hope.

DANA.   For you.

BRAD'S WIFE.   For you, too.

DANA.   There aren't many Brad's in this world ...

BRAD'S WIFE.   But ...

DANA.   You sure are lucky ...

BRAD'S WIFE.   I know that now.

DANA.   You've doubted it?

BRAD'S WIFE.   Oh yes.

DANA.   Well, don't. Ever again. *(Silence.)* You better take me home now.

BRAD'S WIFE.   You're going home?

DANA.   Yes.

BRAD'S WIFE.   But ... ?

DANA.   I feel better.

BRAD'S WIFE.   But what about Alex?

DANA.   He'll get better.

BRAD'S WIFE.   Don't go.

DANA.   He's my husband.

BRAD'S WIFE.   So?

DANA.   I love him.

BRAD'S WIFE.   You can't go back — he'll hit you again.

DANA.   No he won't.

BRAD'S WIFE.   Don't go. We'll find you someone who will love you ...

DANA.   There is only one Brad.

BRAD'S WIFE.   We don't know that. I can check around.

DANA.   *(Smiles.)* Take me home.

BRAD'S WIFE.   Dana.

DANA.   He's got the money, he's got the credit cards. I don't work. I don't know nobody. I got nobody.

BRAD'S WIFE.   You got me.

DANA.   Other than you, I got nobody. Take me home. *(Silence. The lights fade.)*

SCENE 8

Light reveals Brad's Wife looking down on Brad's bed. She sings to him with more love, more feeling than ever before. As she sings, she might lift off her dress. When Brad's Wife finishes singing, she leans over the bed. She might crawl in it or on top of where Brad would be. She giggles. She wipes her eyes. The lights slowly fade.

SCENE 9

The third Sunday. During the coffee hour after the service. Dana and Brad's Wife are sitting at their regular spot.

This week Dana is in much worse shape. She has crutches, her face is bandaged — casts, slings. Band-aids and bruises are everywhere.

DANA.   So it got worse.
BRAD'S WIFE.   You don't even have to say it.
DANA.   It got so bad.
BRAD'S WIFE.   You say it so calmly — you aren't upset?
DANA.   Well, it's almost funny now, almost comical. I mean if you look at it from a certain distance.
BRAD'S WIFE.   But ... ?
DANA.   It isn't funny. No, not one bit.
BRAD'S WIFE.   But I know what you mean.
DANA.   You've been there, I know.
BRAD'S WIFE.   Yes. *(A beat.)* Leave him.
DANA.   Alex?
BRAD'S WIFE.   Yes.
DANA.   Leave Alex?
BRAD'S WIFE.   I think so.

DANA. Sure, of course that's what you think. Most people are quitters. When things get bad, they wrap it all up and toss it in the trash. But Dana Sue Kaye stays. I stay. I'm a fighter. To the final beat of my heart I will fight.

BRAD'S WIFE. But if you go back ...

DANA. What? If I go back — then what? You don't know Alex. In the hospital — we had such a nice talk ...

BRAD'S WIFE. In the hospital?

DANA. Yes — it was like the old days — he was so understanding, so kind. His eyes gentle and sweet. He said "I'm sorry" probably ...

BRAD'S WIFE and DANA. *(At the same time.)* ... a thousand times ...

DANA. ... a *million* times ...

BRAD'S WIFE. Sorry makes it better?

DANA. Sorry is a start! And don't you go judging me or thinking you know better than me ...

BRAD'S WIFE. Dana.

DANA. Not all of us can have what you have with Brad. I mean, come on ...

BRAD'S WIFE. I made some calls. Checked with some agencies.

DANA. What?

BRAD'S WIFE. I've got some news.

DANA. News? *(Brad's Wife extends a picture.)*

BRAD'S WIFE. His name is Todd. He's twenty-seven. Lives in Seattle with his sister and her husband. He's a little longer than Brad. Has more hair. Nice smile, don't you think?

DANA. Yes.

BRAD'S WIFE. He's a Christian. Loves water sports, a voracious reader. Needless to say, he is very interested in meeting you.

DANA. But honey I don't know if ...

BRAD'S WIFE. Dana, there's more. Here is Lars from Sweden. He has no tongue but his father says he is very alert, very positive. Here is Iko from Tokyo. He has a beard which is rare for the Japanese, and he speaks English. He's about the same length as Brad. His only drawback is that he's fifty-two. And

Dana, I found these three in just a matter of days. Give me another week and you'll have plenty of options ...

DANA. You did this for me? *(Brad's wife nods.)* I'm uhm ...

BRAD'S WIFE. You're what?

DANA. Overwhelmed. *Thank you. (Looking at the pictures again.)* I just don't know ...

BRAD'S WIFE. What don't you know?

DANA. No. No no no no no no! No way. Am I leaving. Alex is my. My husband. But thank you. Thank you thank you thank you.

BRAD'S WIFE. Not me, thank Brad. I told him your story. He's been very upset ever since I told him. Every minute practically he's asking about you, wanting to know if everything is alright with you.

DANA. Tell him I'm doing fine.

BRAD'S WIFE. Brad wants me to invite you to live with us.

DANA. No.

BRAD'S WIFE. We've plenty of room, as you know ... and we've got the money ...

DANA. No.

BRAD'S WIFE. So what do you say?

DANA. No!

BRAD'S WIFE. Dana?

DANA. *(Angry.) Why are you so good to me?! You're the nicest thing ever!!! (Dana suddenly turns to audience.) What?!* Oh. I was climbing a tree, yes, Mary Pat. I know it was silly. You only live once, isn't that right? You know how I love trees. You don't? Well, I do. *(Brad's Wife takes the pictures from Dana.)* I did. Well, no I have a ride home ... Alex? Oh honey you know about Alex ... *(Brad's Wife starts to leave.)* Yes ... I know how you like him ... yes ... but he is just one big piece of shit! *(Brad's Wife stops. She looks at Dana.)* That's what he is. Huh? No, I said "shit." *A BIG HEAPING PILE OF WARM STEAMY SHIT!* That's my Alex.

BRAD'S WIFE. We're fine, Mary Pat. Dana is fine. *(Brad's Wife sits back down next to Dana.)*

DANA. *(To "Mary Pat".)* I am, honey. Yes, I am. Things are good. I won't be climbing in trees anymore. Oh no — don't you worry. Everything is looking up for Dana. No more car crashes, no more trees. No more Alex. No more! *(A beat.)* Huh? Oh yes, of course. God bless you, too.

LIGHTS FADE. THE END.

THE VALERIE OF NOW

THE VALERIE OF NOW was produced by Circle Repertory Company (Tanya Berezin, Artistic Director; Connie L. Alexis, Managing Director) in New York City, on February 6, 1990. It was directed by Joe Mantello; the set design was by Loy Arcenas; the costume design was by Laura Cunningham; the lighting design was by Dennis Parichy; the sound design was by Stewart Werner and Chuck London; and the production stage manager was Denise Yaney. The cast was as follows:

VALERIE ....Melissa Joan Hart

CAST OF CHARACTERS

Valerie — twelve

PLACE

Valerie's living room

TIME

Valerie's birthday, 1977

THE VALERIE OF NOW

Valerie sits on a sofa. It's hours before her twelfth birthday party. She is dressed in her birthday outfit and she wears a party hat on top of her head. She holds some Kleenex in her hand. A hand mirror lays by her side.

She is on the phone, in tears. She's in the middle of a conversation.

VALERIE.   K.e.a.n.e. Yes, Keane. Valerie *Keane.* Yes, my mom and dad are coming for my birthday bike. Yes, bike! The Schwinn with the banana seat. If you could tell my mom — just my mom — tell her to call home. V.a.l.e.r.i.e. Just my mom. Tell her to hurry. Oh, forget it. Just forget it! *(Valerie hangs up the phone. She is all alone, frightened and edgy. She dials the phone.)* Mrs. Duffy, may I speak with Kay, please? When do you expect her? Oh. Well, no. No message. Uhm. Mrs. Duffy, you were a girl once, right? OK, when you were ... uhm ... how did you uhm ... never mind, nothing. Tell Kay I'll see her at my party. Nothing, no. Bye. *(Valerie hangs up and waits. She looks at her reflection in the hand mirror. The sound of a group of girl's laughing can be heard. She puts the mirror down fast and dials the phone.)* Janice — it's me. Are you somewhere private? Get somewhere private *fast! (Valerie crosses in back of the sofa, sits behind it. The pointy part of her birthday hat sticks up, the only part of her that is visible.)* OK, Janice. You can't ... OK, Janice? You can't tell anybody what I'm about to tell you. P.r.o.m.i.s.e? You have to. OK, oh boy. I'm vacuuming. I'm home all alone. Mom and Dad went to get my new bike and stuff. And I'm all alone vacuuming when I feel this dripping and I'm thinking I have to pee but the dripping isn't like anything. So I'm walking real fast to the bathroom when I look down and see

... but ... call me back. Eat fast, call me back! *(Valerie throws the phone in the air.) AAAAAAAAHHHHHHHHHHHHH! (She pounds the sofa cushions and thrashes about on the sofa.)* Pull yourself together, Valerie. Keep a lid on it! But will you listen to me? It's affecting me already. My moods are swinging. It's like I'm fine then I want to cry and then I'm happy and then I want to cry and then I'm so looking forward to my party and then I want to ... *(She covers her face with her hands and cries. After a moment, she regains her composure.)* This is unheard of. On your birthday. Taking half a box of Kleenex and uhm having to wedge it in there. But it's so obvious. It looks like I've gained eighty pounds. I look like a pear. Mom. Mom! I want my Mom! *(Valerie hugs a sofa pillow.)* Buck up, Valerie. That's what Dad always says to do. "Buck up." Dad, what does that mean? "Valerie, buck up means — *buck up!*" Thanks, Dad. Thank you for being you. It's sad when you're smarter than those who gave you life. *(Valerie covers her face with her hands again.)* Brenda Palmer believes in destiny. She says that everything happens according to God or somebody's master plan. So wait, let me get this straight, Brenda. You're saying that somebody planned this! Somebody actually sat down and charted out my life and said, "Hey, how's this for an idea? On Valerie's birthday we'll give her a double whammy!" And I'm expected to pray every day. Please. Pray for what? For my life to be over? Cause it's completely ruined, my life. I've been destroyed by nature. Wham. Thanks God. Thanks a total bunch for your most excellent timing! Anybody out there help me?! Helllloooo! Valerie is at home and she's bleeding. And she did the best she could but she's not ready for all the responsibility. She's still a kid. I'm still a kid. I don't even have breasts yet. Aren't you supposed to get breasts first? Monica Mills gets em. She gets breasts — I get blood. I get mood swings, I get forgotten. The phone stops ringing. I lose all my friends. They hate me for being first. "You guys I'm still one of you!" "No, you're not!" "I'm still the same!" "No, you're not! Valerie cut in line!" I have no choice but to hold a press conference. *(Valerie stands on the sofa. She uses her hairbrush as a microphone.)* To Kay, Janice, Brenda and the rest — here is my prepared statement. It happened and it's over and yes, I'm different *but I'm not!* I'm sorry I was first. Please please please please please don't hate me. That'll be all, thank you. No comments. No questions please. No more questions! I think I'm being c.l.e.a.r. Flash. Camera flash. Flash. And the phone starts ringing and ringing. "Hello? Oh, it's OK, Brenda. I would've felt the same." Ring Ring. "Yes? It's OK, Janice, I've missed you, too." Valerie gets all her friends back. And they look hot. And when they go to college, they all live in a houseboat and spend all day in their swimsuits! *(Valerie throws her arms in the air and giggles her glorious, triumphant laugh.)* All the great women through all of history — *Come on down!* Louisa May Alcott, Harriett Beecher Stow! *Marcia Brady!* The question is: How did all you ladies face this moment? Huh? What? It could have been *worse?* Like what? Like I could have been doing cartwheels during recess?! Or like I could've been walking up for my confirmation in my white dress and the Bishop would've looked down. Or *like the party could have been in full swing and I could've been sitting on Kevin Kiernan's lap and whoosh!* *(Valerie sits back to catch her breath.)* Who says you have to tell anybody, Valerie? It can be your secret! Your special secret that makes you glow! But then Betsy Ross and Mary Todd Lincoln and Bat Girl materialize and they say "Go for it, Valerie. Spread the good news!" And so I approach my mom. I hold up the white shorts with the red stain and Mom smiles so big, her teeth uhm grow proud, and uhm tear drops drip and roll down her eyes and we two women look at each other with mutual respect. The tears keep flowing and it's because suddenly she doesn't have a daughter anymore. Suddenly it's like we're sisters. She wants to borrow a bra but mine are too big. We share beauty tips and we do that 'Can you tell which is the mother and which is the daughter' commercial where the hands are shown first. Then, in the backyard where Dad is grilling the hot dogs, he says, "Let me give the birthday girl a hug," but this time he doesn't squeeze the air out of me, he doesn't lift me above him and say, "My little princess" because even he senses the change. It's in my eyes. He shakes my hand and goes back to turning the hot dogs. *(A beat.)* Monica! *Monica!* Oh, hi, Monica. Yes, it's true, I had my period — oh, I don't think any amount of explaining can do justice to what it feels like but know this. For years I've seen your enormous breasts and I've heard you rant about your struggle to find the best bra. Hear this! Maybe you've got the outward shows, the trappings — but me, Valerie, I'm the real woman and you're the f.r.a.u.d. *Fraud! (Valerie sings.)*

"I am Woman
    Hear me roar
In numbers too big to ignore
    And I know too much to go back and pretend
    And I've heard it ..." *

But wait! Six boys bust down Valerie's door. They are sweaty and panting. "Oh, my." They like die at the sight of her. "Hello, have you boys met each other? Well, Chip, I'd like you to meet Chad. Chad, Chip. Tom, this is Tim and Chip and Chad. Bruce meet the boys! Boys, Bruce. Hey, did any of you R.S.V.P.? I don't think so. Sorry, boys. Maybe next year's party." They cry and hold each other. Take them away! Oh, hold all calls. Yes — thank you, Mr. President. Yes sir. It's quite a feeling. What's interesting to me, Mr. President, is that you're a very powerful man and you have enormous impact on people. All people, on history, and you have access to every kind of technology and experts hover around you. You can blow up this world. But you can't know how I feel today, can you? No, I don't think you can. You have no idea of the feeling in *my body.* You have no notion of the enormous power in me today. My baby capabilities. Excuse me, Mr. President, I have a call I must take. Yes, Kevin what can I do for you? Interesting that you'd call in light of today's event. Yes, I know we all change. I allow for that. After all, look at me. Tell me Kevin, where were you before today? I don't recall your asking to carry my milk tray, Kevin, I don't seem to remember any offers to walk me home. But *now* you want to go bike riding,

* See Special Music Note on copyright page.

45

now you want to roller skate. Kevin, go elsewhere! Go find a nice sixth grader! Because Kevin I am the Valerie of Now and now you don't interest me! Kevin, heed these words. *(Spoken.)* "I am Woman. Hear me roar. In numbers too big to ignore. And I know too much. *And I know too much!"** And I deserve better. *(Valerie covers the phone with her hand and looks around.)* Sensing something, the Valerie of Now drops the phone, moves to her balcony and swings open her curtained window. Oh my! She can't believe her eyes. Hello! There are these people — all different races and ages — millions and zillions of people — it's a candlelight procession and helicopters are in the air and planes are skywriting — and boys are hanging from light poles and they're all staring at me like I'm perfect. They're drooling — and there are fireworks and popcorn and dancing in the streets and I raise my hand to speak and there is *silence! (Silence. To the imagined crowd.)* Oh boy. You see, it happens and you're different. Uhm. But you're not, you know? Thank you all for coming to my party! This is the best birthday ever! I will never forget this day! *I will never forget! (Helen Reddy's version of "I Am Woman"** comes up underneath the above text. Valerie is giggling, leaping about on the sofa, her arms extended in victory. As the music swells, the lights fade.)*

THE END

---

* See Special Music Note on copyright page.

PROPERTY LIST

Imagining Brad

2 chairs
Hymnals
Wedding photograph (Brad's Wife)
Purse (Brad's Wife)
2 cups and saucers
Cigarettes
Small table with red-and-white checkered cloth
Arm sling (Dana)
2 empty beer bottles
Beer bottle with beer, open (Dana)
Glass of milk (Brad's Wife)
Crutches (Dana)
Casts (Dana)
Photographs (Brad's Wife)

The Valerie of Now

Sofa
Make-up supplies
Perfume bottles
Party hat
Kleenex tissues
Hand mirror
Telephone
Hairbrush

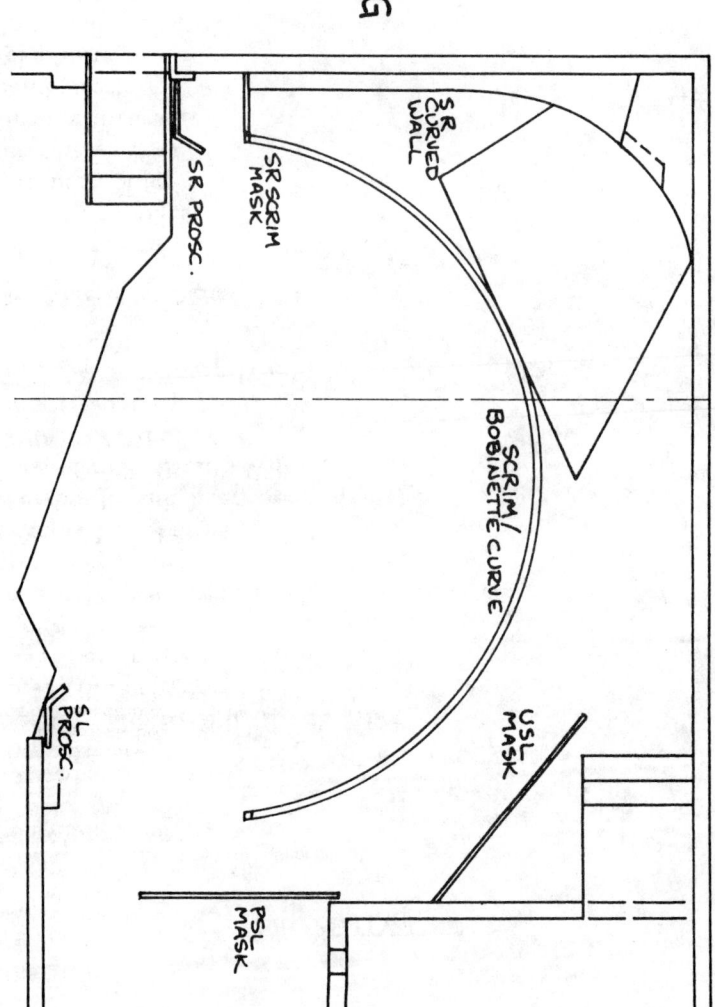

SCENE DESIGN

"IMAGINING
BRAD"

(DESIGNED BY
LOY ARCENAS
FOR CIRCLE
REPERTORY
COMPANY)

SR
CURVED
WALL

SR SCRIM
MASK

SR PROSC.

SCRIM/
BOBINETTE CURVE

SL
PROSC.

USL
MASK

PSL
MASK